Out of Sight Till Tonight!

I'm the Cat in the Hat
and tonight we'll take flight
and meet some of the critters
that come out at night.

The Cat in the Hat's Learning Library® introduces beginning readers to basic non-fiction. If your child can read these lines, then he or she can begin to understand the fascinating world in which we live.

Learn to read. Read to learn.

This book comes from the home of

THE CAT IN THE HAT
RANDOM HOUSE

For a list of books in **The Cat in the Hat's Learning Library**, *see the back endpaper.*

To our grandson Chase, with love

—T.R.

The editors would like to thank
BARBARA KIEFER, Ph.D.,
Charlotte S. Huck Professor of Children's Literature,
The Ohio State University, and
JIM BREHENY,
Director, Bronx Zoo,
for their assistance in the preparation of this book.

Visit us on the Web!
Seussville.com
randomhousekids.com

Educators and librarians, for a variety of teaching tools, visit us at RHTeachersLibrarians.com

Library of Congress Cataloging-in-Publication Data
Rabe, Tish, author.
Out of sight till tonight! : all about nocturnal animals / by Tish Rabe ; illustrated by
Aristides Ruiz and Joe Mathieu. — First edition.
    pages   cm. — (The Cat in the Hat's learning library)
Summary: "The Cat in the Hat takes Sally and Nick to visit with nocturnal animals and to
explore their special adaptations for living in the dark." —Provided by publisher.
Audience: Ages 5 to 8.
Includes bibliographical references and index.
ISBN 978-0-375-87076-7 (trade) — ISBN 978-0-375-97076-4 (lib. bdg.)
1. Nocturnal animals—Juvenile literature. 2. Adaptation (Biology)—Juvenile literature.
I. Ruiz, Aristides, illustrator. II. Mathieu, Joe, 1949– illustrator. III. Title. IV. Title: All about
nocturnal animals.
QL755.5.R33 2015 591.5'18—dc23 2014017837

Printed in the United States of America   10 9 8 7 6 5 4 3 2 1

Out of Sight Till Tonight!

by Tish Rabe

illustrated by Aristides Ruiz and Joe Mathieu

The Cat in the Hat's Learning Library®

Random House 🏠 New York

I'm the Cat in the Hat
and tonight we'll take flight
and meet some of the critters
that come out at night.

So it's time to wake up!
Let's get ready to creep
and see who's awake
while we're all fast asleep.

Nocturnal animals
stay out of sight
during the day
but are active at night.

I wanted to look up
these words right away.

"Nocturnal" means
"active by night."

"Diurnal" means
"active by day."

nocturnal:
nock-**TUR**-null

diurnal:
dy-**UR**-null

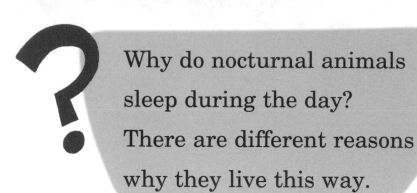

Why do nocturnal animals
sleep during the day?
There are different reasons
why they live this way.

Some hunt after dark
so they don't compete
with diurnal animals
for the same food to eat.

HAWK

OWL

Some prowl at night
to sneak up on their prey.

Some blend in with the dark,
which helps them get away.

To survive, nocturnal animals
have had to adapt
to different conditions
in their habitat.

Their keen senses help them
stay alive through the night.
Some have excellent hearing.
Some see well in dim light.

An aye-aye's big ears
help find food in the dark.
It can hear tasty bugs
moving under tree bark.

ISLAND of MADAGASCAR

A tarsier's big eyes
let in lots of light.
It watches for enemies
that hunt it at night.

ISLANDS
of
SOUTHEAST
ASIA

13

Kiwi birds in New Zealand
can't see very well.
To find food they depend
on their keen sense of smell.

Most animals have
nostrils up by their eyes,
but look at a kiwi—
and you'll get a surprise!

NOSTRIL

Its nostrils are down
at the end of its beak.
It must *sniff* to find food,
since its eyesight is weak.

It takes its long beak
and pokes it around.
It can smell worms
hidden under the ground!

Bats are not blind,
but some have poor eyesight.
So they make high-pitched squeaks
when they're flying at night.

The squeaks bounce off objects,
then back to the ear.
From the sound of the echo,
bats know what is near.

This is echolocation.
It's a form of detection
some bats use to find insects—
their size, shape, and direction.

17

Owls have large ear holes and can pick up the sound of animals moving— even under the ground!

With eyes big and round
to let in the most light,
owls see best when they're
hunting at night.

An owl's flight feathers
let the air pass right through
so it can sneak up
on a mouse or a shrew.

When you ride in a car
and its lights sweep the night,
you might suddenly see
two eyes shining bright.

Some animals' eyes
reflect light, and so
when light hits their eyes,
their eyes seem to glow.

This is called eye shine.
Watch when you're riding
and see if you spot
any animals hiding!

Most animals' eyes
have two kinds of cells.
They are called cones and rods
and they help us see well.

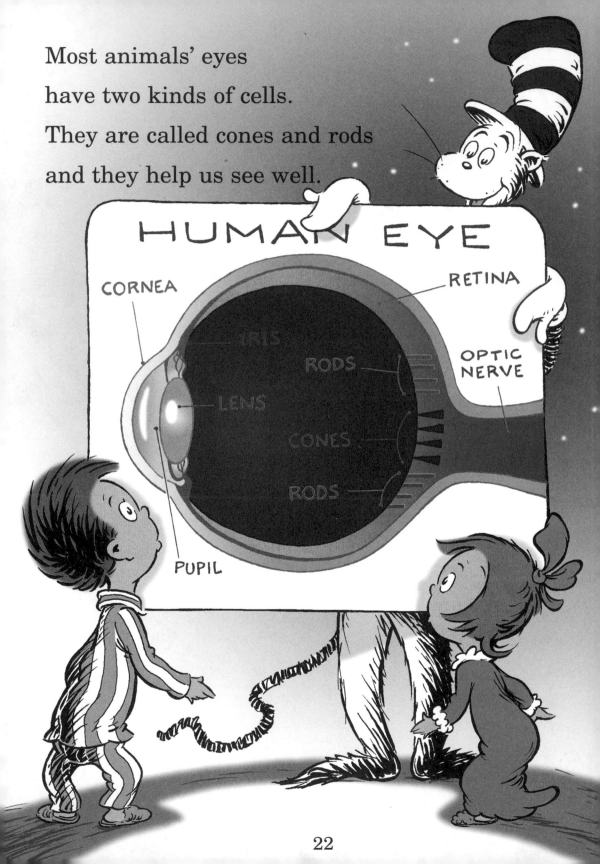

HUMAN EYE

CORNEA

RETINA

IRIS

RODS

OPTIC NERVE

LENS

CONES

RODS

PUPIL

Cones help to see color,
while rods work in dim light.
Animals with more rods
can see better at night.

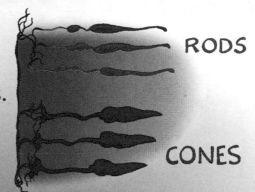

RODS

CONES

Some bats, lizards, and snakes
have no cones, so they
are color-blind.
They see just black and gray.

Raccoons scavenge at night
to avoid enemies.
Their human-like hands
open trash cans with ease.

They eat almost anything
and find food everywhere.
If it's old, moldy, or rotten,
a raccoon doesn't care!

As the moon starts to glow,
if you listen with me,
soon you will hear
a nocturnal symphony!

The night's full of noises.
Wolves start to howl
to let other wolves know
that they're on the prowl.

An owl starts hooting
to say, "I am here!"
He hopes that a female
will hear he is near.

Crickets start chirping.
They chirp and they wait.
Each hopes that his chirping
will attract a mate.

Most toads need to stay damp,
which is one reason why
they avoid the sunlight.
If they dry out, they die.

Toads mate at night
by the light of the moon,
when each male toad sings
his own special tune.

He sits through the night
and keeps singing his song,
hoping a female toad . . .

In the desert, some animals
sleep through the day's heat.
At night they're hungry
and ready to eat.

This banded gecko
hunts through the night.
Its large eyes open wide
to let in the most light.

To protect its eyes
from sunlight during the day,
its eyelids will shut
almost all of the way.

At night in the desert,
a sidewinder sits.
Its body has heat-sensitive
organs called pits.

If a mammal comes near,
these pits feel the heat.
And that's how this snake
can find something to eat!

33

Fireflies flash their lights
to attract mates at night.
They are not really flies—
they are beetles that light.

Each species has a pattern
of lights that they glow.
If a male and female flash
the same one—they'll know!

When nocturnal animals
hunt for food through the night,
they try hard to keep
their babies from sight.

Baby raccoons are called kits.
When they're born, they can't see.
Their mother hides them
in a hole in a tree.

A red fox keeps her pups
hidden safe in their den.
If she senses danger, she'll move them—
then move them again.

A barn owl hides her owlets
in a barn or church steeple
to keep them all safe
from predators and people.

Now dawn is breaking.
The night has gone by.
The sun starts to rise.
The moon fades from the sky.

In a hole in a tree,
in a cave, den, or nest,
nocturnal animals
are now going to rest.

They must hide somewhere safe.

Soon their eyes will be closing.

They've spent the night prowling.

They'll spend the day dozing.

But tonight in a
rain forest, city, or lake,
nocturnal animals will be
blinking . . .

. . . awake!

GLOSSARY

Adapt: To adjust to different conditions.

Color-blind: Unable to see one or more colors.

Cone: A cell in the eye that is sensitive to color and bright light.

Den: The home or shelter of a wild animal.

Detection: Finding information.

Diurnal: Active by day.

Echolocation: Locating objects by making a sound that bounces off them.

Eye shine: The reflected glow in the eyes of some animals in darkness.

Mammal: A warm-blooded animal, living on the land or in the sea, with a backbone, hair on its body, and the ability to make milk to feed its young.

Nocturnal: Active by night.

Organs: Groupings of cells and tissues that perform specialized tasks in an animal.

Rod: A cell in the eye that is sensitive to light but not to color.

Shrew: A small mouse-like, long-snouted mammal.

FOR FURTHER READING

The Bat Scientists by Mary Kay Carson, photographed by Tom Uhlman (HMH Books for Young Readers, *Scientists in the Field*). Follow a team of scientists from Bat Conservation International as they study these amazing—and often misunderstood—animals. For ages 10 and up.

Dark Emperor & Other Poems of the Night by Joyce Sidman, illustrated by Rick Allen (HMH Books for Young Readers). This Newbery Honor–winning picture book combines poems about nocturnal life in a forest with nonfiction passages about the animals in the poems. An NSTA-CBC Outstanding Science Trade Book. For grades 1–4.

Fireflies by Megan E. Bryant, illustrated by Carol Schwartz (*Penguin Young Readers,* Level 3). Includes fun facts about fireflies and suggestions for making your yard firefly-friendly. For ages 6–8.

Owls by Laura Marsh (*National Geographic Readers,* Level 1). A photo-illustrated introduction to owls, written for children just starting to read. For ages 4–6.

Where Are the Night Animals? by Mary Ann Fraser (HarperCollins, *Let's-Read-and-Find-Out Science,* Stage 1). This NSTA-CBC Outstanding Science Trade Book introduces a variety of nocturnal animals and their special adaptations. For ages 4–8.

INDEX

The Cat in the Hat's Learning Library®